GEOGRAPHY *for fun*

Rivers and Seas

Pam Robson

Copper Beech Books
Brookfield, Connecticut

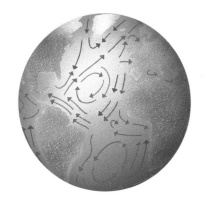

Produced by
Aladdin Books Ltd
28 Percy Street
London W1P 0LD

First published in the United States
in 2001 by
Copper Beech Books,
an imprint of
The Millbrook Press
2 Old New Milford Road
Brookfield, Connecticut 06804

Editor: Kathy Gemmell

Designer: Simon Morse

Illustrator: Tony Kenyon

The author, Pam Robson, is an experienced teacher.
She has written and advised on many books for children
on geography and science subjects.

Cataloging-in-Publication data is
on file at the Library of Congress.

ISBN 0–7613–2421–6

CONTENTS

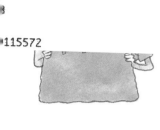

INTRODUCTION

Geography is about people and places and all the changes that take place in the world. How the shape of the land is changed by rivers, especially rivers in flood. How the shape of our coasts is changed by pounding waves. How water can exist as a liquid, as solid ice, and as a gas called water vapor. How pollution in rivers and seas endangers wildlife, which needs clean water to survive. Geography is about all these things. Finding out how we use water will help you understand how important rivers and seas are to life on Earth.

1 Watch for numbers like this. Each step for the projects inside the book has been numbered this way. Make sure you follow the steps in the right order to find out how to make the projects.

MORE IDEAS
● Watch for the More Ideas boxes. They either give extra information about the project on the page, or they suggest other interesting things for you to make or do.

WHAT'S HAPPENING

● The What's Happening paragraphs explain the geography behind the projects you do or make.

● Look in the Glossary at the back of the book to find out what important words mean.

● Use an up-to-date atlas to check where places are.

WARNING

● This sign means that you must take care. Water can be dangerous. Never play beside deep water. Ask an adult to come with you when making observations along river banks or coasts. Also ask an adult to help when you are using sharp tools or hot liquids.

THE SAME WATER

Almost three-quarters of the Earth's surface is water. Most of it is in our oceans or frozen in rivers of ice called glaciers. In warm weather, water evaporates from rivers and seas, which means it changes into an invisible gas called water vapor. When water vapor cools, it condenses, becomes water again, and falls as rain. This is called the water cycle. The amount of water around us stays the same—it just keeps moving through the water cycle.

WATER CYCLE

Make a model to show the water cycle in action. You will need two large plastic bottles, a narrow cardboard box, a craft knife, cardboard, a wire coat hanger, glue, sticky tape, paint, an aluminum foil tray, ice cubes, and hot water. Ask an adult to help you with the cutting, shaping of hooks, and pouring hot water.

1 Draw the outline of a tree-covered mountain slope on one side of the box. Cut around the shape. Paint the outside of the box.

2 Cut a plastic bottle in half lengthwise. Glue one half inside the box to make a river valley. Slide the foil "sea" tray into the box beneath the narrow end of the bottle.

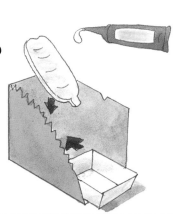

3 Cut the neck off another large plastic bottle. Cut cloud shapes from cardboard and glue them to one side of the bottle.

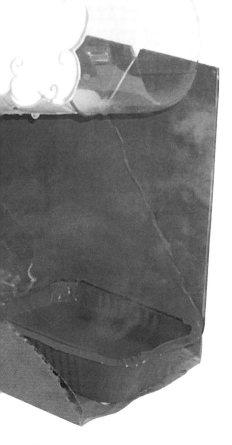

OCEAN DEPTHS
● The largest ocean in the world is the Pacific Ocean. An iron ball dropped into the deepest part, which is over 6 miles deep, would take an hour to reach the ocean floor.

N. America —
Pacific Ocean
— Australia

4 Make hooks from a coat hanger and tape them to the other side of the box, as shown. Rest the bottle on the hooks with its open end facing outward. It should dip at a slight angle.

WHAT'S HAPPENING

● Your model demonstrates what happens in the real water cycle, shown here.

3. The wind blows the clouds toward high land, where the moist air rises and cools even more.

2. As it rises, the water vapor cools and condenses to form tiny droplets, which form clouds.

5 Put ice cubes into the suspended bottle. Pour hot water into the foil tray. Watch the water vapor rise to make "rain" fall from the cloud.

4. The clouds burst and rain falls into rivers, which flow back to the sea.

1. Heat from the Sun evaporates water from seas and rivers.

5. Some rainwater seeps through the land.

FROM SOURCE TO MOUTH

Rivers begin in the mountains. Some start from a melting glacier or lake. Others start as underground springs. Mountain streams are fast-flowing. They erode (carve out) deep V-shaped valleys. As they reach lower land, closer to the sea, rivers flow more slowly. Here, they erode U-shaped valleys as they curve across wide, flat areas of land called floodplains. The natural loop-like curves shaped by a river are called meanders.

MEANDERING AROUND

To show how water likes to meander, you will need sand, a shallow tray, a ruler, a plastic plant trough, wooden blocks, and a pitcher of water.

1 Scoop dry sand into the tray until it is full. Use the ruler, as shown here, to level the surface and remove any extra sand. Make sure the surface is even.

2 Arrange the blocks so that they are higher than the edge of the plant trough. Position the sand-filled tray with one end on the blocks and the other on the edge of the plant trough. Make sure the tray is sloping gently down toward the trough.

3 Gently pour water onto the sand, so that it flows evenly down the slope. Keep pouring steadily. Watch as your "river" changes its course.

WHAT'S HAPPENING

● All rivers make meanders. Meanders curve more as rivers flow over flat floodplains.

● Water flows faster on outside curves and this erodes the river bank. Where the river flow is slower, on inside curves, material that has been carried down the river is deposited (laid down).

Flow is faster and deeper on outside curves. Cliffs form as river banks are eroded.

If a meander becomes too tightly curved, the river flows across the neck of the curve, leaving an oxbow lake.

Flow is slower and shallower on inside curves. Shoals or sand bars form as material is deposited.

Old course of river

Meander

A delta is the low-lying fan-shaped area at the mouth of the river.

Braiding happens where a river becomes a mass of channels. Temporary islands appear. Flooding changes the shape of braiding.

Lip

WATERFALLS

● Where rivers flow over bands of rock that are too hard to be eroded, a waterfall forms. These can be a few feet high, forming rapids, or hundreds of feet high. On high waterfalls, the water spills over the rock at the lip. A deep pool, called a plunge pool, is eroded by rocks and pebbles that swirl around at the base of a high waterfall.

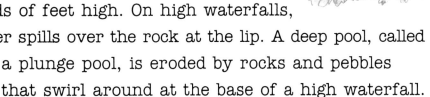

Plunge pool

UNDERGROUND WATER

Water not carried away by rivers becomes ground water. It seeps through cracks and pores (tiny holes) in rocks and collects underground. Rock that soaks up water like a sponge, like sandstone, is called porous rock. Other rock, like limestone, has many cracks and joints for water to seep through. When rainwater, which is slightly acidic, soaks through limestone, it dissolves minerals in the rock and eventually carves out an underground cave. Inside, "icicles" of rock, called stalactites and stalagmites, form from dissolved minerals.

GROWING STALACTITES

Grow some stalactites using a saturated solution of baking soda (see step 1), two jars, a dish, two paper clips, and some yarn.

1 Fill each jar with warm water. Add baking soda to the water and stir. Keep adding soda until no more can be dissolved. This is a saturated solution.

2 Place the jars slightly apart, in a very warm place, with a dish between them. Fasten a paper clip to each end of the yarn. Lower a paper clip into each jar, as shown, so that the yarn hangs over the dish.

3 Now watch the slow growth of a stalactite in the center of the yarn—it will take about a week for a good stalactite to form. Keep a note of how much it grows each day.

WHAT'S HAPPENING

● The soda solution seeps upward, then collects and drips from the center of the yarn. As the water in the solution evaporates, the soda deposit remains and a stalactite grows down from the yarn.

● Stalactites hang down from cave ceilings. Stalagmites build up from the ground. If you leave it long enough, a stalagmite will grow from the water that drips onto the dish.

FLOODING

● Rainwater can seep only so far into the ground. The level at which it stops, where the rock is saturated (can absorb no more water), is called the water table.

● Limestone is permeable rock— it lets rainwater soak through its cracks until the ground beneath is saturated.

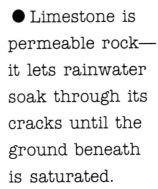

Limestone

Water table

In frequent heavy rain, limestone areas are likely to flood as the water seeps through the rock and raises the level of the water table.

● Heavy rain in mountains is carried downstream in rivers, so floods often happen on floodplains. People build defenses, called levees, to protect their homes.

Floodplain

Major flood level

Flood level
Average river level

Levee

DOWNRIVER

Settlements are often built close to rivers. In the desert area of North Africa, the Nile River provides water for farmers, who grow crops along its banks. The Nile begins as two tributaries, the Blue Nile and the White Nile, which join, then flow northward into the Mediterranean Sea. The Nile is the world's longest river. It is over 4,000 miles long, which is farther than the distance from New York to London.

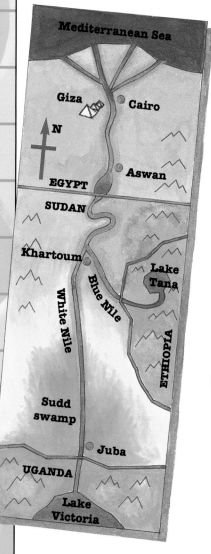

NILE MODEL

A linear map (left) shows important landmarks along a river valley. To make a model of the Nile using this linear map, use a large board, flour, water, newspaper, cardboard, sand, paint, and bottle tops.

Use bottle tops for towns and cities.

1 Find the Nile in an atlas. See if you can spot all the landmarks shown on the linear map. The linear map has no scale. This means that it gives the names of places, but does not show true distance.

2 To make your model, first draw the shape of the Nile onto the board. Then paint it blue. Paint the fertile fields along the river banks green.

3 To make mountains, mix flour and cold water into a thick paste. Tear newspaper into small pieces and soak these in the paste to make papier-mâché. Position small mounds of papier-mâché on the board and shape them into peaks.

Mix sand with yellow paint for the desert.

Make pyramids from cardboard.

When your papier-mâché peaks are dry, paint them.

4 When the painted model is dry, use bottle tops and cardboard to mark the positions of any landmarks, like towns and pyramids. Look at the linear map to find their names, then write neat labels for them.

CROSSING RIVERS

● The first bridge was probably a fallen tree laid across a stream. Now, engineers decide which kind of bridge to build by studying the weight it has to carry and the width of the river.

Suspension bridges are used to span wide rivers or bays. They are supported by cables made from strong steel wires twisted together.

Weight on bridge

Weight spread

A **cantilever bridge** is a balanced structure. Separate cantilevers are joined by short spans of steel.

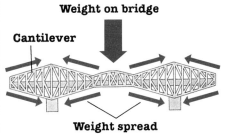

Weight on bridge

Cantilever

Weight spread

An **arched bridge** is a very strong structure, as it spreads weight outward and downward around the whole length of each arch.

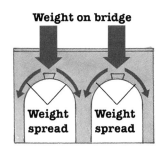

Weight on bridge

Weight spread

Weight spread

RIVER POLLUTION

At its source in the mountains, a stream is sparkling and clear, but farther downstream, human activities cause pollution that reduces the oxygen in the water. Fresh water can become so polluted that plants and animals die. Pesticides sprayed on crops are washed into rivers by the rain. Trash is often dumped in rivers. Waste materials from factories and mines are piped into rivers.

MUDDY FILTER

Our drinking water comes from the water in the water cycle. It is filtered and purified before it reaches our faucets. You can make a water filter using a plastic bottle, sand, water, soil, a paper coffee filter, and a pitcher.

1 Ask an adult to cut the top from the plastic bottle about 4 inches from the lid. Place the top upside down, inside the bottle. Tap it firmly into place.

2 Position the filter paper inside the bottle top. Spoon a layer of sand into the filter. Pour enough water onto the sand to make it wet.

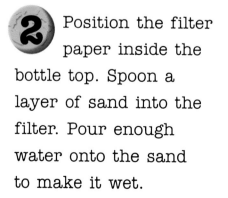

3 Mix soil and water in the pitcher. Slowly pour the muddy mixture onto the wet sand inside the filter. Watch the water pass through the sand and collect in the bottom of the bottle.

4 Now study the water in the bottom of the bottle. It will look cleaner, but beware, it is not fit to drink! Our drinking water is filtered many times before it comes out of the faucet. Compare your filtered water with tap water to see the difference.

POLLUTION DISASTERS

● The Rhine is the longest and dirtiest river in Europe. In 1986, after a fire at the Sandoz factory in Switzerland, more than 30 tons of chemicals entered the Rhine (see right). For 125 miles downstream, all living things in the river died. In January 2000, pollution of the Tisza River in Hungary killed most of the fish within hours.

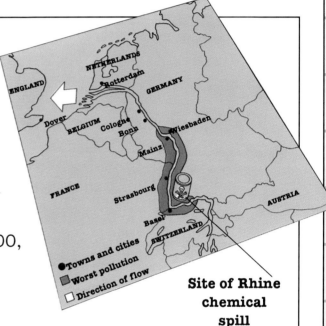

NETHERLANDS
Rotterdam
ENGLAND
GERMANY
Dover
BELGIUM
Cologne
Bonn
Wiesbaden
Mainz
FRANCE
Strasbourg
AUSTRIA
Basel
SWITZERLAND
● Towns and cities
■ Worst pollution
□ Direction of flow

Site of Rhine chemical spill

OXYGEN IN WATER

● Water creatures need oxygen to survive. Much oxygen is released from water plants during photosynthesis, which is the way that plants make food using sunlight. You can test this by putting some Canadian pondweed in a bowl of water. Stand it in the Sun and watch bubbles of oxygen appear.

TOO WET, TOO DRY?

In arid (dry) parts of the world, rain may not fall for months. Rivers stop flowing and soil becomes too dry to grow crops. Farmers need to irrigate their land, which means they supply water to the fields, often through ditches. The ancient Egyptians used an irrigation device called a *shaduf*, which is still used today. Tropical countries have a dry and a wet season. In the wet season, there are sudden, heavy downpours. Sometimes there are floods and drought in the same year.

RAISING WATER

To see how a *shaduf* works, you need a craft knife, corrugated cardboard, tape, a clean yogurt cup, string, a wooden spoon, and clay.

1 Ask an adult to help you cut and fold a strip of corrugated cardboard as shown below. Cut a slot at each end, wide enough for the handle of your wooden spoon.

Fold

2 Tie a long piece of string around the yogurt cup under the rim, as shown, then over the top to make a big loop.

3 Knot another piece of string onto the loop on the cup and tie the other end to the wooden spoon, as shown. Tape a large lump of clay to the spoon.

4 Slot and tape the spoon into the base, toward the clay end, as shown. You may have to add more clay when the bucket is full of water, so that it swings up easily.

5 Place your *shaduf* beside a full sink or basin. Lower the bucket. When it is full, you should be able to raise it very easily by the string. You can now pour the water into another basin.

WHAT'S HAPPENING

● A *shaduf* works as a lever. The clay weight makes it easy to lift the full bucket. In Egypt, water is raised from the Nile and poured into channels to irrigate the fields.

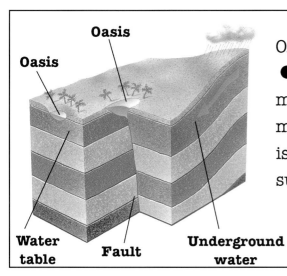

OASIS

● Underground water can seep hundreds of miles through the water table, from distant mountains to low-lying areas. An oasis is where the water table emerges at the surface. This can happen at a hollow in the sand or at a fault, where rock has moved suddenly and a spring appears.

Oasis

Oasis

Oasis

Water table

Fault

Underground water

THE POWER OF WATER

Water power is a clean, renewable source of energy. It has been used for hundreds of years to do work. Water wheels once turned grindstones. Now, water turbines are harnessed to generators that make electricity. This is called hydroelectric power. Huge dams have been built across rivers to provide electricity for cities and towns. However, large dams cause damage to the surrounding land and many people now believe that small dams are better.

WATER WHEEL

To make a water wheel, you will need two large plastic lids, glue, craft sticks, a tray, a craft knife, a plastic bottle, paint, a pushpin, doweling, cardboard, a pitcher, a compass, and water.

1 Ask an adult to pierce a hole in the top of each of the two lids. Glue them together as shown. Now glue craft sticks around the edge of the lids to make paddles.

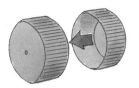

2 Ask an adult to cut V-shapes in the cardboard. Score and fold the cardboard and position around the tray, as shown, to make a support.

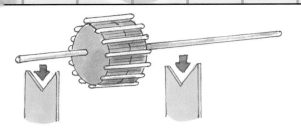

3 Push the doweling through the holes in your wheel, so that one end sticks out farther than the other. Rest it inside the V-shaped notches, as shown.

4 Use a compass to draw a flywheel on cardboard. Cut it out and color brightly. Push a pushpin through the center of the flywheel and into the long end of the doweling.

5 Ask an adult to cut sections from the bottle and glue them together, as shown. Make another support, this time with U-shaped notches and one end higher than the other. Glue on the plastic.

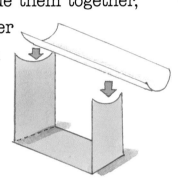

6 Arrange the parts as shown in the photograph. Carefully pour water from the pitcher into the plastic channel. Watch the wheels turn.

WHAT'S HAPPENING

● The energy of the falling water turns the wheel, which spins the flywheel. Raise the pitcher higher, and the added energy in the water will make the wheel turn faster.

● Your flywheel represents a turbine, which drives a generator.

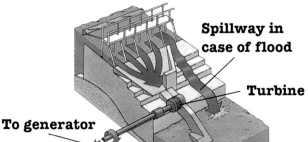

Spillway in case of flood

Turbine

To generator

TIDAL POWER

● Energy from the sea is also used to make electricity. The tide comes in and goes out twice daily. Power stations built across estuaries use turbines that spin in two directions, to harness the tide's energy both as it comes in and as it goes out.

ON THE BEACH

The sea's tides and crashing waves change the shape of our coasts. Tides are caused mainly by the pull of the Moon as it circles the Earth. The pull makes oceans on each side of the globe bulge a little (a high tide) and then fall back (a low tide) every 12 hours or so. Pounding waves and the material they carry cause erosion and deposition. These work together to break down and build up our beaches and cliffs, sometimes forming rocky arches and stacks.

MAKE A COASTLINE

Build a model coastline with a sandy beach to show how waves can gradually wash away the sand from our beaches and form stacks.

1 You will need a long waterproof tray, a pitcher, modeling clay, sand, water, and cardboard. First, shape some tall clay rock stacks and press them firmly in place toward one end of the tray, as shown here.

2 Fill about half the tray with sand, making sure the clay stacks are completely covered. Gently pour water into the rest of the tray.

WHAT'S HAPPENING

● When a part of a wave hits shallower water, it slows down and the rest of the wave bends. When waves reach a headland, they slow, swing around the headland, and hit its sides. This gradually wears it away, leaving a stack or arch.

Headland

Wave direction

Waves bend

Stack formed from old headland

Spit

LONGSHORE DRIFT

● Waves curve and hit bays at an angle. This carries pebbles and sand diagonally up the beach. The wave backwash pulls the pebbles and sand back down the slope at right angles to the beach, gradually moving them along in a series of zigzag patterns. This is called longshore drift. Sand banks and spits are formed this way.

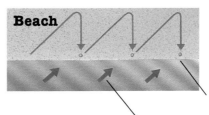

Beach

Sand particle

Wave direction

PEBBLES

● Pebbles are rocks worn smooth by attrition (rubbing against each other) in rivers or seas. They may be flat or rounded, but are always smooth. Shake sugar lumps in a jar. Watch the edges of the cubes rub against each other until they are smooth, like pebbles.

3 Move the cardboard back and forth to make waves. Gradually, the movement of the waves will wash away, or erode, the sand and expose the stacks. You may even see an arch forming between stacks.

WAVES AND WIND

Waves are started by the wind, way out at sea. It whips the water surface into ripples, which build up into waves as the wind gets stronger. The waves get bigger and bigger as they travel through the sea. Although the waves travel great distances, the water in them stays in the same place, moving up and down, until the wave hits a coast. A huge wave called a tsunami can form if there is an underwater earthquake.

TESTING THE WIND

The stronger the wind, the bigger the wave. Test wind strength by building an anemometer. You will need cardboard, a ping-pong ball, a compass, a pen, a ruler, a craft knife, a thumbtack, and glue.

1 Use the compass to draw a curve onto the cardboard. Mark off equal spaces, making a scale for comparing wind speeds.

2 Ask an adult to cut a strip of cardboard with a window, so that you can see the scale. Glue the ping-pong ball to one end.

3 Pin the other end of the strip onto your cardboard scale on the spot where the compass made a small hole. Make sure it can swing freely. Hold your anemometer in a windy spot and see how far the strip is blown.

WAVE MOVEMENT

● If you throw a stone into a pond, ripples form on the surface. A boat will move up and down on the ripples, but not forward or backward. Waves at sea are the same as ripples—they don't move the water forward, only up and down.

● Beneath the waves, water particles move up and down in circles. This causes waves to turn over or break at the surface. When a wave reaches shore, it cannot circulate as well in the shallow water, so it piles up, taller and taller, until it spills over and breaks.

Shore

Wind direction

Wave spills over and moves forward

Water particles

BEAUFORT SCALE

● Storms at sea can drown fishermen and sailors. The Beaufort wind scale (right) was designed for sailors in 1805 by Admiral Sir Francis Beaufort. It ranges from 0 to 12, from calm to hurricane. Force 8 is a gale, force 10 is a stormy sea. Sailors and fishermen listen to the radio for gale warnings before going out to sea.

1 No wind

2 Smoke moves

4 Branches move

6 Crests on water

7 Trees bend

8 Hard to walk

10 Trees uprooted

12 Devastation

OUT AT SEA

Water in the world's oceans is moved around by ocean currents. Near the surface, these currents are caused by prevailing winds, which means winds that occur frequently in certain places. The shape of the land and the ocean floor affect deeper ocean currents. The sea water's temperature and density (the heaviness of a certain amount of water) also affect currents. Very salty water, found in hot, subtropical oceans, is more dense than less salty water, found in cold, polar oceans.

FLOATING FISH

To show that salt makes water more dense, you will need a transparent bowl, salt, a spoon, water, a potato, a pitcher, scissors, plastic lids, and food coloring.

1 Make a solution of salt by adding salt to a pitcher of water until no more will dissolve (about 12 big spoonfuls). Make a note of the amount of water you use. Pour the salt solution into the bowl.

2 Measure out the same amount of water. Add food coloring. Then carefully and slowly pour the colored water, over the back of a spoon, on top of the salt solution in the bowl.

3 Ask an adult to cut a slice of potato about ¹/₂ inch thick. Cut out two fins from the plastic lids and attach them to the potato body of your fish. Place the fish in the water and watch what it does.

WHAT'S HAPPENING

● The fish will sink, then float at the level of the salt water. This is because the density of the fish is less than the density of the salt water, but more than the density of the fresh water.

Fresh water

Salt water

OCEAN CURRENTS

● Currents move in circular patterns and are sometimes called gyres. In the Northern Hemisphere, they spin clockwise. In the Southern Hemisphere, they spin counterclockwise. Some currents are warm and some cold. Ocean currents warm or cool the air above them and this has a major effect on the Earth's weather.

Icy arctic currents meet warm currents from the south

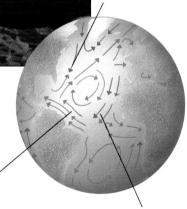

Warm currents

Cold currents

EL NIÑO

● El Niño is an unusually warm current that affects the Pacific Ocean every few years, around Christmastime. It can affect weather all over the world, and is thought to have been responsible for severe droughts in southern Africa, floods in California, and hurricanes in the Atlantic.

Warm water of El Niño moves toward South America

UNDER THE SEA

The gently sloping part of the seabed around the continents is called the continental shelf. It is covered by shallow seas, but is really part of the continent. Sands and gravel in the continental shelf are rich in minerals. A large part of the world's oil and gas deposits are also found under the sea. Oil and gas are fossil fuels, formed over millions of years in layered rock called sedimentary rock. They are found where silt or sand settled on the seabed and buried plant or animal remains. The world's fossil fuels are nonrenewable, which means they will eventually run out.

1. Dead sea plants and animals are buried in sediment that hardens into porous rock.

2. Over years, pressure and heat act on the rock.

They convert the dead plants and animals into oil and gas.

3. Underground pressure forces the oil and gas upward through the porous rock.

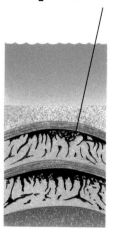

FOSSIL FUEL MODEL

Make a model that shows how fossil fuels are formed. You will need glue, cardboard, scissors, sand, and paint.

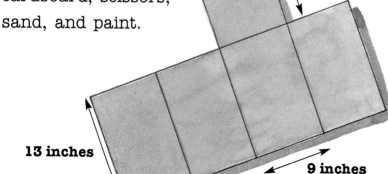

9 inches

13 inches

9 inches

1 Draw the pattern shown here on cardboard. Ask an adult to help you score, cut, and fold it into a long box shape.

2 Paint your box with the layers of sea, rock, gas, and oil shown below. Spread on some glue, then sprinkle on sand to create a realistic effect. Draw and cut out a model oil rig and glue it in position over the oil.

6. Oil rigs drill down to the reservoirs and pump up the oil.

4. The oil and gas reach nonporous rock, which they can't pass through.

5. The trapped oil (black) and gas (green) form underground pockets called reservoirs.

GLOBAL WARMING

● Burning nonrenewable fossil fuels releases polluting gases such as carbon dioxide into the air. World temperatures are thought to be rising because these gases, known as greenhouse gases, are trapping too much heat inside the Earth's atmosphere. This environmental problem is called global warming.

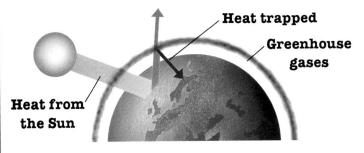

Heat trapped

Greenhouse gases

Heat from the Sun

● Too much global warming will melt the polar icecaps and cause sea levels around the world to rise, flooding low-lying coastal areas. The problem could be reduced if cleaner, renewable sources of energy, like water and wind, were used instead of fossil fuels.

POLLUTION AT SEA

The population of the world is now more than six billion. More people means more trash. Our oceans are now becoming dumping grounds. Polluted water is destroying the food chains of the sea. Oil tanker disasters devastate vast areas of our seas and coasts and kill or harm many thousands of birds, sea mammals, and fish. Scientists use various ways of dealing with the oil spillages. One is to disperse (break up) the oil using chemicals.

OILY WATER

Make some "slick" pictures to see how oil floats and how it can be broken up. You will need a bowl, plastic cups, oil-based paints, turpentine, water, paper, a stick, and dish detergent.

1 Ask an adult to help you mix a few drops of oil-based paint with a little turpentine in a cup. Mix several different colors.

2 Fill the bowl with water. Pour in your paints and stir with a stick to make an oily "slick."

3 Lower a sheet of paper onto the water. Let it soak up the paint, then remove and leave it to dry. Stir the water, then repeat to get different oily patterns.

4 Now squeeze a little dish detergent onto the oily paint, move the stick through it, and watch the "slick" disperse.

WHAT'S HAPPENING
● Oil is less dense than water, which means it floats on top of the water. The detergent splits the oily layer into tiny droplets, which can then sink to mix with the water below.

OIL DISASTERS
● When the oil tanker *Erika* sank off the coast of France in 1999, over 18,000 sea birds with feathers coated in oil were picked up from the oil-covered beaches. In 1989, the *Exxon Valdez* (right) hit rocks off Alaska, spilling nearly 40,000 tons of oil. It polluted 1,200 miles of coastline, killing up to 300,000 sea birds, 5,000 rare sea otters, and many seals and fish.

Exxon Valdez

ALASKA

■ **Damaged shoreline**
■ **Sea bird habitat**
□ **Sea otter habitat**

CORAL REEF DESTRUCTION

● Coral reefs are underwater ridges formed by tiny creatures called polyps. They are only found in warm, tropical seas and are home to an amazing variety of marine life. Coral reefs need crystal-clear water to survive. One-tenth of the world's coral reefs have now been so badly damaged by pollution that they will never recover.

LONGEST, WIDEST, AND DEEPEST

The world's seas and oceans cover 139 million square miles (sq mi). This is more than 70 percent of the Earth's surface area.

The world's largest oceans and seas

Pacific Ocean—64 million sq mi

Atlantic Ocean—32 million sq mi

Indian Ocean—28 million sq mi

Arctic Ocean—5.5 million sq mi

Mediterranean Sea—967,000 sq mi

South China Sea—895,000 sq mi

The world's largest lakes

Caspian Sea (Asia)—143,000 sq mi

Lake Superior (N. America) —32,000 sq mi

Lake Victoria (Africa)—27,000 sq mi

Aral Sea (Asia)—25,000 sq mi

Lake Huron (N. America) —24,500 sq mi

The world's longest rivers

Nile (Africa)—4,160 mi

Amazon (Amazon)—4,049 mi

Yangtze (Asia)—3,964 mi

Mississippi-Missouri (N. America) —3,740 mi

Ob-Irtysh (Asia)—3,461 mi

Huang (Asia)—3,395 mi

Congo (Africa)—2,900 mi

Mekong (Asia)—2,750 mi

The world's deepest ocean trenches

(all in Pacific Ocean)

Marianas Trench—6.85 mi

Tonga Trench—6.72 mi

Japan Trench—6.56 mi

Some of the world's high waterfalls

Angel Falls (S. America) —2,648 ft

Cuquenan (S. America) —2,001 ft

Giessbach (Europe) —1,982 ft

King George VI (S. America)—1,600 ft

Gavarnie (Europe) —1,385 ft

Jog (Asia)—830 ft

Sutherland (Oceania) —813 ft

Tugela (Africa)—597 ft

Victoria (Africa)—354 ft

Niagara (N. America)—177 ft

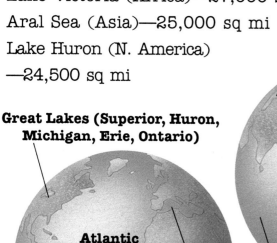

Great Lakes (Superior, Huron, Michigan, Erie, Ontario)

Atlantic Ocean

Caspian Sea

Arctic Ocean

South China Sea

Indian Ocean

Pacific Ocean

Pacific Ocean

Indian Ocean

Mediterranean Sea

GLOSSARY

attrition
The wearing down of pieces of rock carried by wind, water, or ice.

Beaufort scale
A scale from 0 to 12 classifying wind strength.

condensation
The change that occurs when water vapor (a gas) becomes water (a liquid) as a result of cooling.

deposition
The laying down of eroded material carried by wind, water, or ice.

erosion
The wearing down of the land by natural forces such as waves, wind, and rain.

evaporation
When heat causes water to become water vapor (a gas). The opposite of condensation.

fossil fuels
Fuels like coal, oil, and gas formed from the remains of living things.

global warming
A rise in world temperatures as too much heat is trapped in Earth's atmosphere because of air pollution.

ground water
All water that is below the ground.

hydroelectric power
Electrical energy that is obtained from generators operated by water turbines.

irrigation
Any system designed to carry water to the land so that crops will grow.

linear map
A line map showing location and compass direction, not distance.

meander
A bend in a river.

oasis
A source of water in hot desert areas, where the water table reaches the surface.

oxbow lake
A lake left where a river cuts through the narrow neck of a meander.

permeable rock
Rock, like limestone, which allows water to soak through cracks and joints.

porous rock
Rock, like sandstone, which allows water to soak through pores or air holes.

stalactite
A growth of calcium carbonate that hangs from the roof of a cave in limestone rock.

stalagmite
A column of calcium carbonate that grows upward from the floor of an underground cave in limestone rock.

tributary
A small stream or river that joins a main river.

water table
The level of ground water below which the rock is completely saturated.

INDEX

PICTURE CREDITS
Abbreviations: t-top, m-middle, b-bottom, r-right, l-left, c-center.
All photographs supplied by Select Pictures, except for: 4mr, 29bl—Stockbyte.
8ml—Gary Braasch/CORBIS. 10tr, 14m—Corbis Royalty Free. 12mr—Roger
Wood/CORBIS. 16ml—Pat J. Grooves; Ecoscene/CORBIS. 19br—Yann Arthus-
Bertrand/CORBIS. 20mr—Michael Busselle/CORBIS. 23ml—Roger Ressmeyer/
CORBIS. 25mr—Digital Stock. 25bl—NASA. 25bm—Annie Griffiths Belt/CORBIS.